STRAIGHT
SELF DEFENCE

INTRODUCTION

I have read a lot of books on self-defence and martial arts. In these I have found myself reading pages upon pages about the author; their philosophy on self-defence; the history of martial arts; the law; how to run a class and so on.

Now, I've been a fan of martial arts from a very young age and find any practitioners' view fascinating; however I do believe that there is a time and a place for this type of autobiographical style. I have written this book for people that just want to learn a few lifesaving moves. I've tried my best to keep this book as "straight to the point" as I can.

In this book you will learn not only self-defence techniques but key considerations for use in future situations.

This book is not full of overcomplicated moves or deep spiritual in-depth discourse.

This book is straight forward tried and tested techniques with martial artists and non-martial artists that have been used in real self-defence situations.

The techniques discussed here work for me but they may not work for you; I hope that you will find at least one thing in this book that you will say "yes that works for me" but if not, I hope you will learn useful moves which you can adapt to your own needs.

I come across a lot of people that say to me 'I just want to know one good move'... from a punch, one from a kick etc. Well, this is it; this is for the people that may not want to go to the dojo five nights a week and/or go up through the grades/belts but still want to learn some effective self-defence martial art techniques.

Saying this, this book is no substitute for training in a dojo with an instructor or, at the very least, a training partner. To understand how someone else's body moves, you must understand how your body moves and, most importantly, learn to stop someone moving you the way you don't want to be moved.

This takes many years of training and, as the old adage goes, "the more sweat you sweat, the less blood you spill". You need to learn to use your adrenaline to your advantage. With all martial arts and self-defence you need to keep an open mind; use your own experience, watch the techniques used by others and take what you think will work for you, try these techniques and try to adapt them to your benefit to develop your own style.

You cannot be a carbon copy of someone-else if you are two inches taller or shorter, 2lb heavier or lighter; your method of that technique will be different but that doesn't mean they are better or worse. If it works for you that is the important thing. The key is to adapt to every situation and have a defence for anything someone can throw at you.

This book is my take on techniques that work for me and I sincerely hope it makes sense and works for you. If not, change it, adapt it to what will work; this is the journey I've been enjoying for the past twenty years. So, if you're just starting yours or if you are just looking for a new direction, I hope you enjoy this book and will find it to be a useful reference guide which you will return to again and again.

It is important to train with realism in mind and with as much full contact as possible.

Find a good training partner who knows your limits and you of theirs. This type of training will show you what really works. When I'm training people, I like to try this with two or more people. This really gets the blood flowing and will show you how quickly you get closed in and will bring any big headed martial artist back to the ground, usually with a bump.

My very first training was in my local boxing club and then kickboxing so, before I discovered other arts, if I found myself in a difficult situation which led to a physical altercation (otherwise known as a fight) I would box. This is a dangerous approach as one punch can, and does, kill. In this day and age, with CCTV everywhere and camera phones an everyday accessory, punching somebody is a reckless and dangerous thing to do for you and them. It is a funny thing, I know, to be concerned about the welfare of someone who's attacking you, but if you are both unarmed and you hospitalize the attacker, it would most likely be you who may be prosecuted, even though it may be self-defence.

The techniques I use are about control. This could mean using a technique to slow the pace of an attack (diversion or an arm lock to stop an attack); alternatively it could mean controlling the fall of the attacker to ensure that they are not seriously injured (such as a head injury). All self-defence is about control; control of you, control of the situation and control of the attacker. You can do this by following my simple rules.

Important Legal Disclaimer:

The information in this book reflects the author's opinions.

Before practicing anything in this book, first consult a doctor to be sure it's appropriate for you.

The author has made every effort to supply accurate information in the creation of this book. The author offers no warranty and accepts no responsibility for any loss or damages of any kind that may be incurred by the reader as a result of actions arising from the use of content in this book.

The reader assumes all responsibility for the use of the information provided in this text.

CONTENTS

ABOUT ME

I have been studying martial arts for over twenty years now and am an experienced practitioner at black belt level. I have trained with some of the top instructors in my home country and Japan. I've trained in pretty much all of the most popular, and some not so popular, arts. I also train in self-defence classes with lots of practitioners from various backgrounds including security industries. In these classes, we go through real-life situations that have happened. We focus on replicating the things that work, not necessarily those moves which are considered "correct".

I myself have over twelve years' experience of campus security; over the years dealing with big gangs of trespassers, drunks, burglars, drug addicts/dealers, vandals, arsonists and just unhappy aggressive people. The best I feel is when I am confronted with a situation, let's say a group of aggressive people on my own, and am able to influence them without it turning physical. This I have learnt to do over many years using body language and psychology, some of which you will learn in this book.

The very worst thing you can do is match their aggression. This will undoubtedly turn physical and, if you're outnumbered, it will be bad for you. Some situations will turn physical no matter what, train every day so you have the confidence that you will do the best you can looking yourself in the mirror the next day, pretty or not.

THE RULES

The rules in this book I will be referring to are as follow:

1. THE THREE C'S (Calm-Confident-Commit)
2. THE THREE T'S (Talk- Turn- Technique)
3. S.A.F.E (Stance- Avoid- Fight/ Flight/ Freeze- Escape)

These break down as:

RULE 1: THE THREE C'S (CALM-CONFIDENT-COMMIT)

CALM

If you've ever seen someone upset, flailing their arms around in a ball of aggression then you know how ineffective their actions are. Don't let your emotions take over, especially when dealing with multiples; react to an insult aggressively and you will be blindsided by someone else as you're not focusing on what, or who, is surrounding you.

This is the essence of all martial arts- to be calm, controlled and focused. Some people are shocked when you suggest to people that have themselves, or have children, that have been in trouble for fighting or being aggressive, attend a martial arts class. They wrongly believe that it will only fuel their behaviour.

In reality, and I've seen this first hand, lots of time someone that is aggressive, tense and unfocused will soon find out this is the wrong path. They will do one of two things- get frustrated and not return or change.

CONFIDENCE is key!

If you show weakness, others will exploit it. Move with confidence; let them know you are no push over. But be careful, don't jump in to a karate (or other type) stance; I've seen people go down hard by making this mistake. You want to be defensive but passive.

Finally, COMMIT!

If you have to defend yourself, commit to whatever technique you're doing. If you half commit to a strike or technique because you're afraid it won't work, it won't. Have conviction in all you do.

Stick to one or two simple moves. When dealing with multiples, the key is to create space and not to get tied up with one attacker. This also could mean you have made an opening to get the hell out of there. COMMIT to it! Take the opportunities and literally run with it.

RULE 2: THE THREE T'S (TALK- TURN- TECHNIQUE)

TALK

If you can TALK your way out of there, do it. Remember, language is the best defence you have. It can also be a powerful weapon.

If dealing with multiple attackers, for example, you should direct this to the ringleader(s). You will know who this is, whether from their actions or the body language of those around them. If it turns physical, this is also the one who you should engage first. The rest should back off once the ringleader has been defeated. I've seen this happen on many occasions, although you can never depend on this.

TURN

It is easy for an attacker or group of people to manoeuvre you into a position you do not want to be in. You do not want to be pinned against a wall or in a corner. You need to talk and turn. Try this slowly, your conversation may prove distraction enough to move them around and you could even put them in the position you were just in, and possibly get out of there.

TECHNIQUE

A lot of martial artists have too many techniques to call upon and this can fluster them. You need to keep it simple. In a closed in situation, especially with multiples, locks are out! Use the space gaining techniques which we will go through in the next pages; learn to take advantage of space and then get the hell out of there.

RULE 3: S.A.F.E (STANCE-AVOID-FIGHT/FLIGHT/FREEZE-ESCAPE)

STANCE

It's no good keeping your feet together. If you get hit, you'll go down. Keep a centred posture.

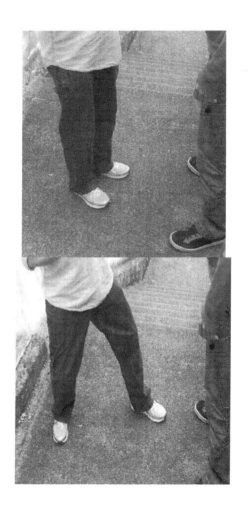

Stay out of reach. One inch can be the difference from someone giving you a clean punch or an awkward one. In picture one below; the attacker can get a lot of power

17

from his shoulder and a quick punch from his left. Note: Only move to the point that they won't turn to face you again. From the position in picture two, you have a much better chance of seeing and reacting to an attack.

FIGHT, FLIGHT OR FREEZE

One of the body's most primitive and reactive actions is the "fight/ flight/ freeze response" which prepares the body to "fight" or "flee" from a perceived attack, harm or threat to our survival. When our fight or flight response kicks in, various chemicals, including adrenaline, are released into our bloodstream. This can cause dramatic changes to your body. Your respiration increases. Blood is re-directed into our muscles and limbs in anticipation of running and fighting. Your body will react to stimuli in a different way- survival is your goal and to do this it stops interpreting pain (as pain would slow you down). This reaction has been attributed to many feats of extraordinary strength and stamina. A heightened sense of awareness prepares your body to react in whatever way will ensure your survival.

By learning to recognize the signals of fight flight freeze you can learn to utilise the benefits of your body's responses without being disadvantaged by other aspects. Being able to focus your attention in extreme physical and/ or emotional situations will enable you to do what is necessary- run faster, fight harder, last longer.

But at this point we must remember to also use THE THREE C's (CALM, CONFIDENT, COMMIT).

To freeze in a dangerous situation is also part of your body's natural response. This could save your life but, for a self-defence situation, this is not a desirable state. Some people more than others will freeze but with training you can bring yourself out of this.

Lots of things can trigger the fight/ flight/ freeze response, not just immediate threat to life. Something as simple as a loud noise can be a trigger. This is why a lot of people suffer from stress and why I think it is important to have a good release routine.

Every day, as part of my fitness regime, I do half an hour on a punch bag then I run for half an hour. This is releasing the build-up of chemicals because I am fighting and fleeing. I believe martial arts are a great way of releasing this, and also learning how to control it.
To do this is an art all in itself.

ESCAPE
Look for openings to escape. Create openings by using THE THREE T's. The key to surviving a situation like this is not to be the best martial artist on the planet; the key is just to take advantage of the mistakes that an untrained individual will do.

From 2011-2012 in the UK, there were over two million incidents of violent crime reported. With the introduction of expensive mobile phones and such street crime has been on the up yearly.

So, now let's learn how to keep you and your family safe.

THE WARRIOR CREED

BY ROBERT L. HUMPHREY

Wherever I go, everyone is a little bit safer because I am there. Whenever I return home, everyone is happy I am there. Wherever I am, anyone in need has a friend.

THE CHECKLIST

Having a check list to go through when under the pressure of a possible attack will calm the mind, keep you focused and remind you of all your training and how to keep safe.

Imagine the scenario... you are a security guard doing a check around the site you are protecting. You turn a corner to see four or five undesirables on your site. Your aim is for them to be gone as quickly as possible without incident... Not easy.

The check lists I use change according to the situation but are adaptable to every situation.

RULE 1: THE THREE C'S (CALM - CONFIDENT – COMMIT)

Calm

At this point, you need to keep your cool- not running away and not running at the gang either.

Confident

Being confronted by more than one attacker can be a very scary experience but it is also the time to not show it.

Commit

In this case committing is not wavering in your conviction. You are telling them to leave and they have no other option. You need to believe this yourself or it will show in your voice and body language.

Use the best weapon you have... your brain!

RULE 2: THE THREE T'S (TALK– TURN- TECHNIQUE)

You may be able to TALK and TURN the gang. Distance is important- too close and you could get hit; make sure no one gets behind you keep everyone in sight. Your hope at this point is that they leave; job well done!

We will say, for this example, they don't and someone strikes you so you need to use a TECHNIQUE.

And finally:

RULE 3: SAFE (STANCE- AVOID- FIGHT/FLIGHT/FREEZE- ESCAPE)

Choose a STANCE; AVOID the attack, FIGHT back and ESCAPE get the hell out of there. When dealing with multiples distance is your friend so let's get started with a space gaining technique.

TRAINING TECHNIQUES

SPACE GAINING TECHNIQUE

As an attacker comes in from the right, bring your left arm up to cover your head. Now bring a short kick up to groin level, always remembering THE THREE C's.

The kicks in this book are going to be quick and short range, there will be no roundhouses.

You need to think of any kick as an extra punch or a good distraction- if it doesn't connect, this is fine- you are creating space.

At this point, the attacker should have buckled over enough for you to move to strike the side of head/neck. Always use side of the hand, never strike/punch with your knuckles as you can easily break bones. Remember, one punch can kill. Many people spend life in prison from throwing one punch; every technique here is about control. The strike should be directed at the same time as you put your foot down from the kick using gravity force. This directs the attacker away from you.

Next follow through back to the normal position.

SUMMARY

Keep a cool head- use THE THREE C's.

Posture stance and balance is everything- keep S.A.F.E (STANCE- AVOID- FIGHT- ESCAPE)

Space is the key and you need to get it any way you can. See a bit of wood/ a metal pole; use THE THREE T's (TALK- TURN- TECHIQUE) to get to it. I've even seen someone take off their belt and start swinging! To gain the space they needed to run off this worked. I always carry my keys on a chain, this is legal and I train with it every day.

KNIFE ATTACKS

I have in the past trained with lots of knife experts, the best being a Royal Marine Commando whilst training in Japan. I have also had real life experience with knife attacks. Many people I have trained and spoken with have experienced this type of attack too. There are lots of differing views on knife attacks so this is my view. So, again, try things out, train and see what works for you.

What I have discovered is that if your attacker knows how to use a knife well realistically, if you have no weapon, you will GET CUT. To what extent is down to your training and reactions.

If you're engaged in an unarmed fight you would expect to get punched. Well, as easy as it is to punch you, if someone has a knife it is just as easy stab you. This is a recurring theme, with people I've spoken to; they didn't even realize it had happened until the fight was over. They believed it was a punch, only to discover that they'd been stabbed. Again, this is possible when you are in your fight and flight mode. Adrenaline will mask the pain, this is something to watch out for- there are good and bad sides to adrenaline.

Your hope though, is that your attacker is untrained and/or is using the knife for intimidation. Now, they may not intend to use it but this is a chance you cannot take. Your mind should be focused on being SAFE, with emphasis on ESCAPE- this could well be the first thing you do, run and get away from the danger. This may not be possible; if you have your family with you, for instance.

Knife attacks are where THE THREE C's (CALM CONFIDENT COMMIT) really come in to play: being calm is not easy I know; stay confident and, more than on any other technique, you need to COMMIT. If you do not commit to a move when you are in an unarmed attack, you might get punched but still get away with it. But if you half-heartedly attempt a move here, you may not be so lucky with your life.

This is why, whatever you're going to do, do it with full force whether it be on your toes out of there or executing a technique.

TALK TO A GUN; SHOUT AT A KNIFE

If someone is pointing a gun at you, the last thing you want to do is shout at them. A nervous person with their finger on the trigger should be spoken to very very softly.

In reverse, you should shout at someone with a knife! If they are not expecting it, their natural reaction is to flinch and pull away; this will move the knife towards them, not at you which is what you want. Move fast and move in, this will give you more of a fighting chance.

KNIFE DEFENCE- TECHNIQUE

Responding to a knife attack is all about timing. You need to practice this. Move too soon and they'll pull back before attacking again. Move too late and you are in trouble.

I see a lot of people in dojos really afraid to get a technique wrong and instructors moving in as soon as they see it and berating students. This just frustrates students. This is not how I teach or train; I encourage students to get it wrong before they can get it right. I will tell them to move out too early, or too far, or too late or too close. That way they understand what will happen when you get it wrong, see the whole picture and get it right.

Find your right way in your own time. You can't practice timing and distance enough; explore every combination so, when the real time comes, you'll know what to do.

If you have to block, use the outside of your arms. This protects your main arteries. This can be an unnatural block so practice this.

If the attacker is waving the knife at you from a relatively safe distance and you think you can commit and succeed, punch or kick the knife hand to send the knife flying. Now the hand should be weakened and you can take them down using some of the techniques in this book.

If this does not release the knife and they're still waving it around, I believe you need to get two hands on their knife hand. It's not often we say grab, let alone grab with both hands, but in my view and with the knife training I have done, you have to use two hands on the knife hand or they will snatch their hand back. At this point, you may get punched with their other hand but it's the price you pay for control of the knife and, if you act fast, the fewer punches you will take.

You've blocked with the outside of your arms now grab their arm with both hands and, at the same time, twist their arm over so their elbow is pointing up; this will make it a lot harder for them to pull back.

Move your left arm so your armpit is just over their elbow, keeping their elbow up and both of your hands on that grip.

Squeeze down, keeping their arm up and the shoulder down.

Next, give a kick to the head; now as I've said a punch or a kick can kill but if someone is attacking you with a weapon you need to do anything you can to disarm the attacker.

Always remember, if you feel resistance and the technique is not going on, don't fight. Move in the opposite direction. This is what separates the good from the bad. I have seen lots of people trying with every ounce of being to put a move on that's not working when they should have switched. This is the real key to self-defence- switch and switch again! Whatever technique you do, try to go an opposite way and then move from one to the other. The in-between is what we refer to as the flow.

SUMMARY

When unarmed and confronted with a knife you need to use as much force as necessary. A lot of people will say control the mind then take the weapon and, I agree with this to an extent, but you cannot rely on this. I believe you need to get rid of the weapon as soon as you can. Do not mess around; surprise can be a powerful thing!

Use THE THREE C's (CALM CONFIDENT COMMIT) - commit to that knife flying across the room. If you can't get rid of the weapon, you must weaken their hand. Don't hurt yourself by trying to punch them in the head. Hurt them by punching their hand; it's very hard to stab someone with a weakened hand. Remember to train with reality in mind but understand that in reality a lot goes out the window. The most important thing is to practice movement. I have seen people train with live blades; not something I recommend. A good alternative are some old white t-shirts and some red marker pens.

DEFENCE FROM A KICK

There are two ways to defend from a kick- block/counter kick or redirect. In both instances, you will have to move and move instantly or you'll feel the full force.

As said in the last chapter, someone that knows how to kick is very very hard to defend but it is not impossible.

I have sparred with very skilled kickers, including British Tai Qwan Do champions and the problem you will have is that kicks are fast. If you cannot whip a kick in fast and stay centred, you shouldn't do it. This is because this will 1) put you off balance and 2) be easily defended against. In my experience, sparring with advanced kickers, the key is to move fast (always with SAFE in mind) and keep your elbows at the ready- elbows are not a kicker's friend.

Luckily for you, though, you're not likely to meet someone that's been kicking all their life on the street.

I find that a kick from an untrained person will come in from the outside at thigh level or below. Most peoples' experience with kicking is a football so it's this kind of arch.

Where kicks are, I think, the most dangerous (and what I want to address first) is when you find yourself on the ground. This is where, to the untrained, your head becomes the football. We've all seen sickening footage on the news of people getting kicked and stomped on when on the ground. Next to facing a knife or a gun, I believe this is the most dangerous place to be.

Training on the ground for this reason is important. The biggest problem for beginners to martial arts or self-defence is that they are afraid to go down to the ground. This is a natural reaction because, since you were a toddler, you've been trying to stay on your feet. So, when you take a beginner to the ground for the first time, their body will become rigid so they will hit the floor harder. Once on the floor, it is more difficult to move which is why I will spend a lot of time with beginners on break falling and rolling. I dedicate a lot of my training to ground work and regularly train in a Brazilian Jiu-jitsu class, one of the best ground fighting arts you can find. I want to feel confident that if a fight goes to the ground, I can either get up quickly or take control.

I see a lot of people in training halls and their mind is somewhere else. When they are thrown to the ground, they aren't thinking about what is happening to them, they are just waiting for their next turn. To me, these people are half training. When someone does a technique on me and I go down to the ground, I will either get up quickly keeping my eyes on my attacker at all times or use something I call the "block and up".

BLOCK AND UP TECHNIQUE
(Or 'How to get up effectively')

You're on your back on the ground.

When your attacker comes in at you, move your body so your feet are facing them.

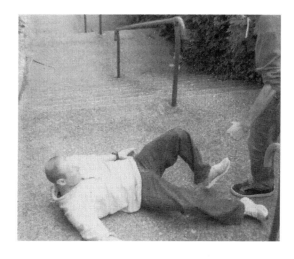

Pull your left foot in to your bum and your left hand up.

Push your right arm onto the ground and the right leg in the air to protect your body.

Next, swing your right leg as far back as you can between your right arm and left leg and stand up.

I try to do this every time and can't believe when I see people turn their back to get up. Do this on the street and you're in trouble.

LEG TAKE DOWN (FROM KICK ON THE GROUND)

Now let's look at what you can do if you've no time for the 'block and up' and a kick is coming in to your head.

A good exercise is just to lie on your back moving your body using your arms and legs. This will build the muscles you will need to move affectively on the ground.

You're on the ground and a kick is coming in.

Bring your arms immediately up to guard your head as kick comes in. From your left side, cup their ankle with your left hand.

Bring their foot to your chest. This will prevent them pulling their foot back.

With your right arm, push just below their knee outwards direction and they will go down.

When they land, watch their feet, protect yourself, get up and escape. It is very important to train this over and over again from all angles. You'll be using muscles you didn't even know you had.

This same technique will work standing up as if the kick was coming in at waist height. On the street, you will not find many people that can effectively kick higher.

STANDING KICK DEFENCE

Now this time you are standing and a kick is coming in from the left.

Move away from the kick, as you would the same as riding a punch; that way if it does connect, it's not as powerful.

As before, with your left hand cup their ankle and this time clasp it to the side of your body.

With right arm, as before, put pressure down and out just below the knee. This will work but, if they won't go down for some reason, you can sweep the other leg. Doing this will mean they hit the ground harder and possibly on their head so calculate your move. Be careful with training partners and attackers. Remember one blow to the head can kill.

DEFENCE AGAINST A FRONT KICK

As a front kick comes in, move back enough to take the power out; block by crossing your arms down and as close to your body as possible.

Bounce off this block, move straight in and take down.

OUTSIDE DEFENCE KICK

You've managed to move soon enough and you can redirect the kick coming in.

Next, step in with your right leg. This will move their kick out further than if you had allowed the leg to hit the ground naturally. This will put them off balance and ensure they have their back to you. Stay in as close as you can get, watching out for their elbows and take them down.

SUMMARY

Kicks are very dangerous and hard to defend from people that know how to kick; keep a good guard using your elbows.

If you find yourself on the ground use the BLOCK AND UP. On the ground, you lose half of the movement you would normally have, which is the same as if you were up against a wall; this makes you vulnerable to kicks from all angles.

If you can grab a kick, take them down fast; don't keep hold. Twist the heel in and the knee out and they will go down. Move to either create distance or close distance; don't make it easy for them.

DEFENCE FROM A STRAIGHT OR HOOK PUNCH

To defend a punch, you will need to get very close to the punch and not move too soon or you will be in a 50/50 boxing contest.

I have trained with a lot of beginners who are afraid of being hit. This is, of course, natural but will not help you in a self-defence situation because they all seem to do the same thing- go very tense and squish there head into their shoulders and close their eyes waiting impact.

To be effective in self-defence, we need to lose the fear. This will take time because the best and safest way to do this is by building up slowly. It's not just fear that's the problem, there are good martial artists out there that have never been in a fight and have never really got hit so will not understand how their body will react.

You start to do this with techniques that involve a punch being delivered to a specific part of your body. Get your partner to start off slow until your body is conditioned to take a harder punch. Do the same with some light sparing and build it up over weeks/months.

If you don't have a training partner, use your environment; for example, trees have been used for body conditioning for hundreds of years.

As in any technique, to be able to defend well you should be able to do well and punching is no exception. Here are a few tips on punching:

Where does the power come from?

It's not the arms or shoulders; it's the hips and the legs. Stand on one leg and try to push someone back they won't move. Put that other leg down and bingo, there's the power. They will move. So the same is true with a punch, it's all from the legs.

Stay relaxed. Focus on THE THREE C's. Tense your body up and you will not be able to use speed. Speed and power (the power coming from the legs) equals a good punch.

Keep your elbows in and your wrist straight. A mistake people will make is to throw their elbow out and then snap their forearm forward. By doing this, all of the power is going away from the body and out from the elbow, not forward from the arm. The wrist should be kept straight or also you will lose power or worse, you could break your wrist.

DEFENCE

As far as defence goes, I'm saying we need to stay close, have no fear, always remember to stay SAFE and get under the punch or stop the punch coming back in.

DEFENCE FROM A PUNCH 1

First, let's stop the punch coming back in.

When a punch is coming in from their right, keep both arms up.

If you have time, move your left forearm straight to punch their bicep whilst keeping your right arm up in defence.

If you're in closer, use your elbow.

This will ensure the punch will not come in again. The harder they throw their punch in, the more a punch to the bicep will hurt. Try it as the attacker and then see how hard you throw it in the second time.

DEFENCE FROM A PUNCH 2

Let's try an over the head block.

With this technique, get as close as you can whilst defending the punch; this will stop the attacker from gaining space, pulling their punch back and throwing it back in again.

A right hook or straight punch is coming in. Keep your guard up.

Use your left elbow to redirect the punch over your head. This should be practised a million times, left and right until it becomes second nature automatic. To do this you need to get your muscles to remember and there is only one way to do this- repetition.

At this point, don't let them go; stay close. You should now be on the right of their body.

On this side it will be impossible for them to do you any damage. With your right forearm strike down on their right forearm, this should buckle their body over.

Keeping your right arm in contact with their body, slide up to the head with your left arm and, at the same time, push their hip out and they will go down.

SUMMARY

Learn how to punch well; this will give you a good understanding of how to defend. It's no good defending well but being unable to stop them coming back in with more punches; sooner or later you will get caught. This is not a competition; this could be life or death. The tools they're using in this instance are the arms. Break the tools and close the distance. Get sparring, get a punch bag, use the correct stance and get that muscle memory working for you.

HEADBUTTS

Head-butts are commonly seen in fights on the street. It is not something a skilled practitioner in self-defence would usually do unless there were no other options and it is not the first thing you would do. Remember, control is the true skill so you can be assured that if they are coming in with the head butt; they've got nothing else in their arsenal.

The problem with head-butts is that they can come in fast and take you off guard and be very dangerous. What you see a lot is the double grab 'push and pull' to the head- it's the whiplash action that nine times out of ten will

61

knock you out. Always be ready for it. A head-butt can be the very beginning of a fight, we've all seen the two people squared up to each other arms wide apart about a centimetre apart then boom the head-butt comes in and starts or finishes the whole thing. Don't let this happen to you.

DEFENCE TECHNIQUE FOR A HEADBUTT

The grab is going to be the first contact.

As soon as you feel the grab, punch down on both hands.

Bounce off of the hands and straight into a palm strike to the face. Don't worry if the grab stays on, it's the head-butt you want to stop.

Alternatively, the uppercut is one of the best punches you can master. The uppercut is short and powerful and usually is a knockout punch because it's not easily seen. It's the punch you don't see that will knock you out. But remember, you don't always want to punch this can leave you with a broken hand. Using the bottom part of your palm is just as good.

Train yourself to throw the uppercut as you're being pushed back. If you get the timing right, as they grab you to throw the head butt in, their head has to go down to strike you on the top of their head. As their head goes down, that's the time to whip in the uppercut and knock their head back.

SUMMARY

The head butt is one of the most dangerous attacks you will come across on the street.

Be ready for it; it's going to come in fast and hard and it can be the only thing they do or need to.

The grab is more than likely to be the first thing you will feel. As an exercise, get your training partner to push you on the left and right side and, with every push, get used to your arms going up to protect your head.

DEFENCE FROM A BEHIND GRAB

The grab from behind is something that could be done to hold you, or maybe to slam you on the floor or even to bundle you into a car in a kidnapping for instance.

We will look at grabs that can come under your arms over your arms or around the neck.

SITUATION 1: UNDER THE ARMS

If they're grabbing you under the arms, they will be grabbing lower on the hips. Your arms are free so use your elbows. You know where their arms are so you will roughly know where the rest of their body is. Put as much force into your action as possible!

SITUATION 2: OVER THE ARMS

There are two ways to deal with this before they lock the arms.

Before:
As soon as you feel their arms around you, explode your arms out.

Push your bum out, which will make them bend.

Now strike with the back of your head. If this doesn't connect, it's ok as they'll have moved back and you have the room to escape.

After:
If your arms are locked up, they won't be able to lock your forearms below the elbows. Put your knuckles on to the back of their hands, then grasping with your other hand push down on the back of your hand. If this does not release the grasp, it will give you room to move under their arms and away.

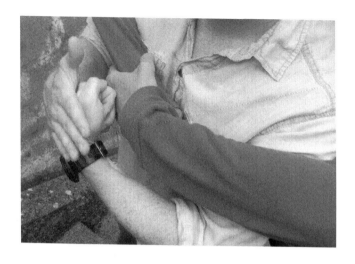

SITUATION 3: 'AROUND THE NECK' CHOKE

You are being choked with their right arm around your neck. As soon as you feel the hold going on, get your chin down. Or pull down on the arm and tuck your chin in. If they get their arm under your chin, you will be a lot easier to move and control. Someone putting a choke on is looking to crush your windpipe, to cut the blood supply to the brain so you will pass out, or to control you to the ground or to pull you somewhere. Getting your neck down will give you a bit of room. You can still get choked out but will give you a little more time.

Now with their right arm around you, reach up with your right and find their left hand- they'll be using this to support their choking arm. Grab the fingers of their hand if possible.

Pull their left arm up and over the back of your head.

Next with your left arm, put it over their left to stop the arm going back around your neck.

Let go of the fingers with your right hand and slide it up your body under the attacker's arm and to the right of your chin.

When their arm releases from your neck and you have the room, elbow their ribs with your right arm, turn and you're out of the choke.

SUMMARY

If someone gets you in the right position and under the neck, it is nearly impossible to get out of and you can be out cold in seconds, especially if they are taller and bigger than you.

They will try to get a better leverage advantage over you. Don't let this happen. They want their arms tight around your neck. Don't let this happen.

Think S.A.F.E (STANCE- AVOID- FIGHT/FLIGHT/FREEZE-ESCAPE). Take your stance and don't let them arch your back. Avoid their body, they want you close. Turn on their fight or flight by pinching their arm, grab flesh and make them want to escape. Escape when there's enough

73

space that you can step into it, under their arms and now you have their leverage. You only have a few seconds to do all this a good idea is to put a ten second timer on when training. If you're not out by then, start again.

DEFENCE FROM AN OVERHEAD ATTACK

The over the head attack means the attacker will have something in their hand such as a bottle or pool cue.

If you see the attack coming in, you can react quickly. Step in and block their forearm with your forearm **only if the attacking arm is not lower than their chest**. If it is, you're too late and their arm will go through your block.

You've blocked with your left to their right; with your right hand go on the outside of their arm and put your thumb in the crease of the elbow joint.

Now pull your right hand towards you holding their right wrist and your left forearm away from you. Control their wrist with your right hand this will also protect you from their left punch. Control them to the floor making sure they cannot turn their body into you.

OUTSIDE DEFENCE OF OVERHEAD ATTACK

You've blocked as defence one with your forearm but you've left it too late or they're too strong to put the second part on, don't fight it, and go with it.

With your left hand on their right, step to the outside of arm, let the arm go down, get your arm on top of theirs without losing contact and pin their bottle arm to your body.

With your left hand, move to the left of their head and pull in to your chest.

Turn your hips in with an elbow strike to the head with your right.

DEFENCE AGAINST A BASEBALL SWING

For this you will need to move fast- move in fast or step back fast.

As the swing goes back, both arms are at this point to one side of their body.

Move in and cover the arm closest (their left arm if they're doing a right arm swing). Cover above the elbow so they can't move their arms. Now they have lost all power in the swing.

Reach across their body keeping control of the arm closest to you at all times. Take the bat and the arm across your body. It's ok if they do not let go of the bat, you are in the controlling position and have a lot of options.

Alternatively, wait until they have swung. This takes a lot of speed and timing, get it wrong and you know the rest. A good tip is to keep your feet still and move your torso towards the attacker. This gives the illusion you are closer. When they swing you have a better chance to move out the way.

After the bat has missed you move in fast and hard.

Do not wrestle with the bat, but give it a pull towards you the idea is not to disarm but to off balance them then go straight for the head. When people hold on to weapon, it's very hard for them to let go, like a kid with their hand stuck in the sweet jar because they won't let go of the sweets. This means they have lost two of their weapons; their hands and the bat as at this point are behind you.

Go for the head to control or strike after they have lost balance. Watch and go to disarm; there will be no power behind a swing but a connection could still do some damage.

SUMMARY

When someone has something in their hand to swing at you, speed and timing are everything; just stand there and it's goodnight. Use THE THREE C's- be CALM, CONFIDENT and COMMIT. If you hesitant and don't move in, this will give them space and that means they will keep coming. If you meet resistance, don't fight it; let it go, move out of danger and control.

CLOSE QUARTERS

DEFENCE 1

Close quarter training is vital training and not a lot of people think about it but a lot of attacks do happen in confined spaces such as toilets, buses, trains or alleyways.

Someone is attacking you and you can't get any power behind any strike. A good defence is a double strike to the ears. This can daze an attacker (note, this can burst the eardrums so be careful when training). You should have some time to follow up with some close combat elbow strikes.

85

DEFENCE 2

Their head will be in close and a head butt is a real threat.

Step to their outside left as much as you can. With your right hand, push their left cheek right. They will fight against this and push towards you. When the time is right go with it, scoop your hand around the back of their head bringing it to left elbow

SUMMARY

It's a good idea to train as close as you can, practice this as much as you can. If you're up against a wall you can still use THE THREE T's (TALK- TURN- TECHIQUE) and, ideally, have the attacker against the wall.

DEFENCE FROM A SEATED POSITION

A seated position is quite a vulnerable one. You could be sat in a car, waiting for a bus, at the movies on a bar stool or even at work so training for this is well worth while.

SITUATION 1:

A double grab comes in as you're sat down. Keep your hands up.

Bring them down to you, don't go to them.

Stand up keeping control of the head twisting the neck up.

Finish with a strike to the head.

SITUATION 2:

You're in your car and the attacker puts their arm through your car window to grab you or your keys.

Grab their arm and pull them towards you.

At the same time, using your other arm, elbow the attacker to the head.

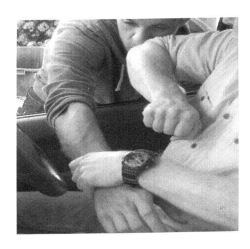

You are pulling the attacker on to your elbow; this should daze them and give you sufficient time to get away.

The advantage you have here is leverage, as you do in a judo throw, say. A lower centre of gravity can be to your favour.

SUMMARY

If you're sat down, it's going to be a sudden attack- one you're not expecting because, if you are expecting something, you're best to get up. This may, in some instances, stop the attack coming in. If not and you have stood up, move away from whatever you were sitting on because you may end up sat back down and still getting attacked. If this is the case, you haven't gained anything and worse, you could fall completely over the top.

Do one or the other; stay seated bring them to you or, if you have the time, get up. If you meet the attack half standing, you will be off balance.

If, for instance, you're in your car, it is very difficult to get up and out quickly. You could be grabbed, dragged out of your car and the car stolen. Or you could possibly be subject to an attack from the passenger side. So number one rule is keep your car doors locked, especially when sitting in a queue or at the lights.

BOOK SUMMARY

Self-defence is different to any martial arts in a dojo; no-one in a dojo is really trying to inflict harm upon you. I have talked to people that, like me, have trained most of their lives and, when it came to a real life encounter, the training went out of the window or they ended up rolling around on the floor, standing in a clinch or being assaulted and not being able to do anything. This is reality, this is the street.

In reality, anyone with no training whatsoever can get a lucky punch, an unseen strike and win a fight. You just need to use the instinct to fight that we all have. If you understand this, you can train with the mind-set that everyone is dangerous and every move is dangerous; prepare for anything and everything, this is self-defence.

Fighting is the last resort; think about THE THREE C's (CALM- CONFIDENT- COMMIT), THE THREE T's (TALK- TURN- TECHIQUE) and S.A.F.E (STANCE- AVOID- FIGHT/FLIGHT/FREEZE- ESCAPE) from this book and use them. So remember to be confident, stay calm, talk your way out of the situation if you have time, physically turn yourself, have a good stance, use the adrenaline of your fight and flight and escape out of there. Doing these things will act as signals to the people around you and hopefully the attackers will subconsciously take this in and this could influence them into not attacking.

It is my wish that someone was to read these principles and it helps them avoid a physical confrontation altogether.

If you have no option but to fight, stay calm, confident, talking and turning but then commit to a technique. Have simple techniques in mind; not necessarily the examples I show in this book, but one or two from each attack that works for you and I hope this book is a good starting point. Everyone should have some form of self-defence that works for them in mind because one day they may wish they had.

Many thanks for reading. Stay calm, stay safe and be happy.

Simon Hunt

Please take a minute to leave a review on Amazon letting me know if you have learned from this book.

Copyright © 2014 by Simon Hunt

Printed in Great Britain
by Amazon.co.uk, Ltd.,
Marston Gate.